Bird Shirts

by Trisha Roberts
illustrated by Kersti Frigell

Core Decodable 49

McGraw Hill Education

Bothell, WA • Chicago, IL • Columbus, OH • New York, NY

MHEonline.com

Send all inquiries to:
McGraw-Hill Education
8787 Orion Place
Columbus, OH 43240

ISBN: 978-0-02-143419-0
MHID: 0-02-143419-0

Printed in Canada.

9 10 11 12 KOD 24

The girls had gifts for Amber.

Her first gift was a shirt.
The shirt had a bird on it.

Amber's next gift was a shirt.
It had a bigger bird on it!

Amber's third gift was a skirt.

Amber's last gift was a shirt.
Was there a bird on it?

As a matter of fact, there was!